M000117116

This journal belongs to

_____

Copyright © 2018 Inna Perelmuter
All righs reserved
No part of this publication may be reproduced, stored in a retrieval system or transmitted
in any form or by any means, electronic, mechanical, photocopying, recording or otherwise,
without prior writen permission from the author.

https://www.amazon.com/author/inna.perelmuter
https://www.amazon.com/author/smartkidspress

Are you a good friend? Why do you think so?

_____

_____

_____

_____

_____

_____

_____

_____

_____

_____

_____

_____

_____

What is something that makes your family special?

_____

_____

_____

_____

_____

_____

_____

_____

_____

_____

_____

_____

_____

What age is a person an adult? Why do you think so?

_____

_____

_____

_____

_____

_____

_____

_____

_____

_____

_____

_____

_____

_____

If could change one rule that your family has, vwhat would you change?

_____

_____

_____

_____

_____

_____

_____

_____

_____

_____

_____

_____

_____

_____

Of all the things you are learning,
what do you think will be the most useful
when you are an adult?

_____

_____

_____

_____

_____

_____

_____

_____

_____

_____

_____

_____

_____

How would the world be different if animals could talk?

_____

_____

_____

_____

_____

_____

_____

_____

_____

_____

_____

_____

_____

_____

Would you cheat on a test if you knew you would not get caught? Why or why not?

_____

_____

_____

_____

_____

_____

_____

_____

_____

_____

_____

_____

_____

_____

What is the best gift you have ever given?
Why was it so special?

_____

_____

_____

_____

_____

_____

_____

_____

_____

_____

_____

_____

_____

_____

What is the hardest thing about being a kid?

_____

_____

_____

_____

_____

_____

_____

_____

_____

_____

_____

_____

_____

_____

If you were a teacher, and the kids in your class
would not listen to you, what would you do?

_____

_____

_____

_____

_____

_____

_____

_____

_____

_____

_____

_____

_____

_____

Date _____

Where is your favorite place in the world?

_____

_____

_____

_____

_____

_____

_____

_____

_____

_____

_____

_____

_____

_____

If you could give one gift to every single child in the world, what gift would you give?

_____

_____

_____

_____

_____

_____

_____

_____

_____

_____

_____

_____

_____

_____

Date _____

If you could travel back in time three years and visit
your younger self, what advice would you give yourself?

_____

_____

_____

_____

_____

_____

_____

_____

_____

_____

_____

_____

_____

_____

What ten words most describe you?

_____

_____

_____

_____

_____

_____

_____

_____

_____

_____

_____

_____

_____

_____

What do you think would be the hardest thing about being blind?

_____

_____

_____

_____

_____

_____

_____

_____

_____

_____

_____

_____

_____

_____

If you could make one rule that everyone in the world
had to follow, what rule would you make? Why?

_____

_____

_____

_____

_____

_____

_____

_____

_____

_____

_____

_____

_____

When was a time that you felt angry?

_____

_____

_____

_____

_____

_____

_____

_____

_____

_____

_____

_____

_____

Date _____

What is something you would have liked to do differently today?

_____

_____

_____

_____

_____

_____

_____

_____

_____

_____

_____

_____

_____

_____

What makes someone a good friend?

_____

_____

_____

_____

_____

_____

_____

_____

_____

_____

_____

_____

_____

_____

When was a time that you felt impotent?

_____

_____

_____

_____

_____

_____

_____

_____

_____

_____

_____

_____

_____

_____

What would you change about school?

_____

_____

_____

_____

_____

_____

_____

_____

_____

_____

_____

_____

_____

Date _____

What do you like about yourself?

_____

_____

_____

_____

_____

_____

_____

_____

_____

_____

_____

_____

_____

When was a time that you felt excited?

_____

_____

_____

_____

_____

_____

_____

_____

_____

_____

_____

_____

_____

_____

What's the silliest thing that happened today?

_____

_____

_____

_____

_____

_____

_____

_____

_____

_____

_____

_____

_____

_____

Date _____

What is/was your favorite thing to do during recess?

_____

_____

_____

_____

_____

_____

_____

_____

_____

_____

_____

_____

_____

_____

when was a time that you felt creative?

_____

_____

_____

_____

_____

_____

_____

_____

_____

_____

_____

_____

_____

_____

Date _____

Was there anything that happened today that made you feel bad?

_____

_____

_____

_____

_____

_____

_____

_____

_____

_____

_____

_____

_____

Which playground skill do you plan to master this year?

_____

_____

_____

_____

_____

_____

_____

_____

_____

_____

_____

_____

When was a time that you felt motivated?

_____

_____

_____

_____

_____

_____

_____

_____

_____

_____

_____

_____

_____

_____

What is one thing you hope to learn before the school year is over?

_____

_____

_____

_____

_____

_____

_____

_____

_____

_____

_____

_____

_____

What rule was the hardest to follow today?

_____

_____

_____

_____

_____

_____

_____

_____

_____

_____

_____

_____

_____

When was a time that you felt mad?

_____

_____

_____

_____

_____

_____

_____

_____

_____

_____

_____

_____

_____

_____

When did you feel most proud of yourself?

_____

_____

_____

_____

_____

_____

_____

_____

_____

_____

_____

_____

_____

_____

What is one thing you did today that was helpful?

_____

_____

_____

_____

_____

_____

_____

_____

_____

_____

_____

_____

_____

_____

Date _____

What was your favorite subject to study today? Why?

_____

_____

_____

_____

_____

_____

_____

_____

_____

_____

_____

_____

_____

_____

If you had the chance to be the teacher tomorrow, what would you teach the class?

_____

_____

_____

_____

_____

_____

_____

_____

_____

_____

_____

_____

_____

What would you rate your day on a scale of 1 to 10? Why?

_____

_____

_____

_____

_____

_____

_____

_____

_____

_____

_____

_____

_____

_____

What challenged you today?

_____

_____

_____

_____

_____

_____

_____

_____

_____

_____

_____

_____

_____

Date _____

What new fact did you learn today?

_____

_____

_____

_____

_____

_____

_____

_____

_____

_____

_____

_____

_____

_____

Date _____

Who made you smile today?

_____

_____

_____

_____

_____

_____

_____

_____

_____

_____

_____

_____

_____

_____

Date _____

What was the nicest thing you did for someone else?

_____

_____

_____

_____

_____

_____

_____

_____

_____

_____

_____

_____

_____

Date _____

What was the funniest thing that happened today?

_____

_____

_____

_____

_____

_____

_____

_____

_____

_____

_____

_____

_____

Date _____

What is your favorite book?

_____

_____

_____

_____

_____

_____

_____

_____

_____

_____

_____

_____

_____

_____

What is your favorite superhero and why?

_____

_____

_____

_____

_____

_____

_____

_____

_____

_____

_____

_____

_____

What is the best thing abour your life?

_____

_____

_____

_____

_____

_____

_____

_____

_____

_____

_____

_____

_____

_____

Date _____

What can you do to be a better child?

_____

_____

_____

_____

_____

_____

_____

_____

_____

_____

_____

_____

_____

_____

What do you want to be when you grow up?

_____

_____

_____

_____

_____

_____

_____

_____

_____

_____

_____

_____

_____

_____

Date _____

What is your bigest wish?

_____

_____

_____

_____

_____

_____

_____

_____

_____

_____

_____

_____

_____

_____

What is your bigest summer memory?

_____

_____

_____

_____

_____

_____

_____

_____

_____

_____

_____

_____

_____

_____

_____

Date _____

What was the best day of your life?

_____

_____

_____

_____

_____

_____

_____

_____

_____

_____

_____

_____

_____

Date _____

Do you want to grow up and get married? Why or why not?

_____

_____

_____

_____

_____

_____

_____

_____

_____

_____

_____

_____

_____

_____

What is your favorite Holiday?

What do you like doing?

_____

_____

_____

_____

_____

_____

_____

_____

_____

_____

_____

_____

_____

_____

What do you like about your mom?

_____

_____

_____

_____

_____

_____

_____

_____

_____

_____

_____

_____

If you could do anything rigth now, what would you do?

_____

_____

_____

_____

_____

_____

_____

_____

_____

_____

_____

_____

_____

_____

_____

Date _____

What is a memory that makes you happy?

_____

_____

_____

_____

_____

_____

_____

_____

_____

_____

_____

_____

_____

_____

Date _____

What scares you?

_____

_____

_____

_____

_____

_____

_____

_____

_____

_____

_____

_____

_____

What is the funniest joke that your friend has told you?

_____

_____

_____

_____

_____

_____

_____

_____

_____

_____

_____

_____

_____

What is your favorite sport? Why?

_____

_____

_____

_____

_____

_____

_____

_____

_____

_____

_____

_____

_____

_____

Date _____

What do you like dream about?

_____

_____

_____

_____

_____

_____

_____

_____

_____

_____

_____

_____

_____

_____

What do you like about your dad?

_____

_____

_____

_____

_____

_____

_____

_____

_____

_____

_____

_____

_____

_____

_____

What do you look forward to when you wake up?

_____

_____

_____

_____

_____

_____

_____

_____

_____

_____

_____

_____

_____

If you opened a store, what would you sell?

_____

_____

_____

_____

_____

_____

_____

_____

_____

_____

_____

_____

_____

_____

_____

Date _____

What makes you fell loved?

_____

_____

_____

_____

_____

_____

_____

_____

_____

_____

_____

_____

_____

_____

How do you feel when you mom is hugging you?

_____

_____

_____

_____

_____

_____

_____

_____

_____

_____

_____

_____

_____

If someone gives you $100, how would you spend it?

_____

_____

_____

_____

_____

_____

_____

_____

_____

_____

_____

_____

_____

_____

What do you enjoy giving people?

_____

_____

_____

_____

_____

_____

_____

_____

_____

_____

_____

_____

_____

If you wrote a book, what whould it be about?

_____

_____

_____

_____

_____

_____

_____

_____

_____

_____

_____

_____

_____

_____

Date _____

What do you think you're going to dream about tonight?

_____

_____

_____

_____

_____

_____

_____

_____

_____

_____

_____

_____

_____

_____

Date _____

What makes you feel thankful?

_____

_____

_____

_____

_____

_____

_____

_____

_____

_____

_____

_____

_____

_____

Date

If you could grow up to be famous,
what would you want to be famous for?

_____

_____

_____

_____

_____

_____

_____

_____

_____

_____

_____

_____

_____

_____

Which area of your school is the most fun?

_____

_____

_____

_____

_____

_____

_____

_____

_____

_____

_____

_____

_____

_____

Are you afraid of anithing?

_____

_____

_____

_____

_____

_____

_____

_____

_____

_____

_____

_____

_____

_____

If you could be invisible for a day, what would you do?

_____

_____

_____

_____

_____

_____

_____

_____

_____

_____

_____

_____

_____

_____

Which person in your class is your exact opposite?

_____

_____

_____

_____

_____

_____

_____

_____

_____

_____

_____

_____

_____

what is better – swimming in the pool or the ocean?

_____

_____

_____

_____

_____

_____

_____

_____

_____

_____

_____

_____

_____

_____

_____

Where would you like to travel?
How would you get there?

_____

_____

_____

_____

_____

_____

_____

_____

_____

_____

_____

_____

_____

_____

If you could invent something that would make life easier for people, what would you invent?

_____

_____

_____

_____

_____

_____

_____

_____

_____

_____

_____

_____

_____

_____

Date _____

What is you learned about a friend today.

_____

_____

_____

_____

_____

_____

_____

_____

_____

_____

_____

_____

_____

_____

What would you do if you made the rules at home?

_____

_____

_____

_____

_____

_____

_____

_____

_____

_____

_____

_____

_____

_____

When was a time that you felt lucky?

_____

_____

_____

_____

_____

_____

_____

_____

_____

_____

_____

_____

_____

_____

Who do you want to make friends with but haven't yet? Why not?

_____

_____

_____

_____

_____

_____

_____

_____

_____

_____

_____

_____

_____

_____

Which of your friends is the best listener?

_____

_____

_____

_____

_____

_____

_____

_____

_____

_____

_____

_____

_____

_____

You are outside for a whole day: what would you do?

_____

_____

_____

_____

_____

_____

_____

_____

_____

_____

_____

_____

_____

_____

If you could be anyone for a week, who would you be? Why?

_____

_____

_____

_____

_____

_____

_____

_____

_____

_____

_____

_____

_____

Date _____

What is your favourite weekend activity?

_____

_____

_____

_____

_____

_____

_____

_____

_____

_____

_____

_____

_____

Date _____

What makes you fell brave?

_____

_____

_____

_____

_____

_____

_____

_____

_____

_____

_____

_____

_____

_____

When was a time that you felt silly?

_____

_____

_____

_____

_____

_____

_____

_____

_____

_____

_____

_____

_____

What do you think would be the hardest thing about being parent?

_____

_____

_____

_____

_____

_____

_____

_____

_____

_____

_____

_____

_____

How do you show your famaly members you care?

_____

_____

_____

_____

_____

_____

_____

_____

_____

_____

_____

_____

_____